Recipes for Healthy Living

50 YOGI TEA® Recipes & Yoga-Postures

FSC	MIX Paper from responsible sources FSC® C002544	ClimatePartner ° climate neutral Print | ID: 10307-1307-1006

YOGI TEA GmbH
Burchardstraße 24 • D-20095 HAMBURG
info@yogitea.eu • www.yogitea.eu

Index

Dressings

Main Dishes

Desserts

A wonderful tea can be the whistle in a fantastic dish!

YOGI TEA® introduces a truly inspired book of recipes, created with YOGI TEA® blends. "Recipes for Healthy Living", is a new and unique recipe book that is sure to delight all, using healthy plant based ingredients without compromising on flavour or enjoyment. "Recipes for Healthy Living" is a perfect cook book for people who want to introduce more fruits and vegetables into their diet.

"Recipes for Healthy Living", includes over 50 pages of inspired recipes and 50 yoga sets to support a fresh, vibrant holistic lifestyle.

Our inspiration comes from Ayurvedic principles of using spices in everyday meals. Traditionally spices are known to give each dish its unique flavour, refining it with colour, sharpness, character and digestibility. Yogi Bhajan's YOGI TEA® creations use spices as the healing heart of each recipe. We use over 77 different spices in our YOGI TEA® range. Spices are known throughout the world as being the lifeblood of a delicious, lively cuisine.

Celebrate the limitless creativity in your kitchen.

Please wait at least one hour after eating to do any of the yoga exercises in the book.

Founding Father

In 1969, Yogi Bhajan came from India to the West and began to teach Kundalini Yoga, meditation and Ayurveda. After his classes he would serve an aromatic spice tea to his students, which the affectionatley named "Yogi Tea".

Today YOGI TEA® has grown to a range of over 45 highly specalized Ayurvedic recipes designed to support vitality and well being.

"Amid the swirling, confusing, unfocused energies of the modern world there is a light, calm and healing in the center of all things."

Yogi Bhajan, Master of Kundalini Yoga

Ayurveda – the ‚science of life'

Ayurveda is a practical and philosophical way of life from ancient India that prescribes conscious living as a key to a balanced and long life. Through the Doshas Vata, Pitta and Kapha, the elements manifest in a unique combination in every being. To maintain that individual balance in one's life is the foundation of Ayurveda. In ayurvedic nutrition the six taste qualities are of major importance.

Our herbal, spice and fruits infusions are so balanced in their taste profiles that their enjoyment helps to maintain the perfect balance in your daily busy lives. These light full-flavoured mixtures of timeless wisdom allow your inner potential to unfold in harmony, letting your spirits rise.

The three Doshas

*According to Ayurveda, the entire universe is divided into five elements. These elements combine with each other and give rise to the three forces that are fundamental to our life. In our bodies, these forces are known as the three „Doshas" **Vata (V) Pitta (P) Kapha (K)**. Each one of us has our own unique combination of Doshas from birth throughout life, which is called „constitution". Typically one or two Doshas predominate, although some of us have all three in equal proportion. The basic key in Ayurveda is to maintain the same relative proportion of Doshas in your innate constitution. This balance is synonymous with health, vibrancy and your experience of well being and happiness. A Dosha produces specific effects both when in balance and out of balance.*

Doshas & Qualities	Dominant in Season	Balanced Characteristics	Imbalanced Characteristics
Kapha	moon / rain	**mind:** love, nurturing, compassion, patience	**mind:** greed, envy, holds grudges, attachment
Energy of FLUID AND STRUCTURE Qualities: cold, heavy, wet, static, dull, dense	Last days of winter / Beginning of spring	**body:** builds, nourishes, lubricates, protects, fluids, reproduction	**body:** congestion, obesity, allergies, lethargy, respiratory
Pitta	sun / heat	**mind:** intelligence, memory, discernment	**mind:** anger, hate, controlling, hot temper
Energy of TRANSFORMATION Qualities: hot, sharp oily, light, mobile, smooth	Last days of spring / Summer	**body:** metabolism, digestion, eyes, skin, brain & heart	**body:** acid, heart burn, acne, hypertension, nausea, migraines
Vata	wind	**mind:** creative, spiritual, tranquility	**mind:** fear, anxiety, stress, worry, poor memory
Energy of MOVEMENT Qualities: dry, cold, light, rough, mobile, subtle	Autumn / Early winter	**body:** blood, flow, nerve impulses, fast in actions	**body:** hyperactivity, dry skin, constipation, gas, arthritis

Beetroot Muesli Crunch

Takes 30 minutes | makes 4 portions

Ingredients

100 grams of beetroot pulp, 1 ½ bags of **YOGI TEA®** Licorice (contents), 50 grams oat flakes, 50 grams buckwheat grains

Preparation

Take the pulp* you are left with after juicing beetroot and add contents of the YOGI TEA® Licorice tea, mix well. Spread out lightly on baking paper lined oven tray. Bake in a preheated oven at 180°C for 30 minutes. Stir a few times while it is baking. Remove from the oven and let it cool. Toast the oat flakes and buckwheat grains in dry skillet until light golden brown. Let the buckwheat and oat flakes cool. Once they are cool add to the baked beetroot crunch.

*Tip: *Beetroot pulp is used from Beetroot Coconut Soup.*

Ayurvedic Info: V-P-Ko

To Wake Up

Sit crosslegged with your spine straight and bring your forearms parallel to the ground. Make fists of your hands and stretch your thumb straight up. Make the arms stiff from the shoulders to the tip of the thumb. Shake your whole body vigorously for 3 minutes. The breath is flowing automatically. Keep focus on the tip of the nose.

Please ask your doctor if this exercise is suitable for you.

Love and Compassion are the anchor of life.

Overnight Balancing Oats

Takes 5 minutes (+ overnight soaking) | makes 4 portions

Ingredients

100 – 160 grams rolled oats, 200 ml hot water, 4 bags of **YOGI TEA®
Women's Balance**, 200 grams of banana, 160 grams (approximately
4 big handfuls) blueberries, 160 grams (approximately 4 big handfuls)
raspberries, 4 medjool dates (without the pit)

Preparation

*Steep the YOGI TEA® tea bags in hot water (100 °C) for 7 minutes and let it
cool. Once cool add banana to the tea and use a hand mixer to make into
a smooth liquid. Chop dates into fine pieces. Add date to the banana tea
mixture. Divide oats over 4 jars. Add one forth of the banana tea mixture
to each jar. Add one handful of blueberries and one handful of raspberries
to each jar. Close with lid and let sit in fridge overnight. Remove from the
fridge 15 minutes before severing to serve at room temperature. Serve with
a little fresh mint.*

Ayurvedic Info: V-PoK+

Yoga for Mental Clarity

Sitting cross-legged, rest your right
hand on your knee. Block your left
nostril with your thumb. Breathe slowly
and deeply through your right nostril
only, eyes closed. Focus on your breath
for 3 minutes. Sit up straight, take a few
deep breaths and relax.

Please ask your doctor if this exercise is suitable
for you.

Only who loves himself, can share love with others.

Detox Porridge

Takes 15 minutes | makes 4 portions

Ingredients

200 grams millet, 20 dried apricots (cut into strips),
800 ml almond milk, 2 pods of vanilla, 4 bags of
YOGI TEA® Detox (contents), the zest of 1 orange

Preparation

Place millet, apricot strips and almond milk into a pan. Scrape the vanilla pods and add to mixture for baking. Heat the pan on and cook on low heat for 15 minutes. Add YOGI TEA® Detox (contents) and cook for 1 minute. Remove from heat. Sprinkle the zest of 1 orange on top.

Tip: *Add some extra almond milk, almond slivers and fresh figs before serving.*

Ayurvedic Info: V-P-Ko

Break-fast

Simple Yoga to Refresh Yourself

Sit straight. Create hooks with your hands and then lock them together at chest level. Keep lower arms parallel to ground, twist upper body and head first to the left, then to the right. Inhale as you turn to left; exhale as you turn to right. 1–3 minutes.

Please ask your doctor if this exercise is suitable for you.

Speak to your soul.

Rose Blueberry Muffins

Takes 30 minutes | makes 4

Break-fast

Ingredients

Dry ingredients: 100 grams whole rice flour, 40 grams arrow root, 60 grams grated coconut, 1 teaspoon of guar gum, 12 grams of baking powder, 4 pinches of sea salt

Wet ingredients: 240 grams of ripe banana, 80 grams of blueberries, 2 – 3 bags of **YOGI TEA® Rose** (contents), 40 grams (= 2 large) of medjool dates (without the pit), 4 tablespoons of rice syrup

Preparation

Combine the dry ingredients in a bowl. Mash the banana, and add the contents of 2 to 3 bags of YOGI TEA® Rose then add the remaining wet ingredients to the dry ingredients. Stir well. Place mixture in a muffin tin. Bake in a preheated oven at 180°C for 25 minutes. Remove from oven and let cool.

Ayurvedic Info: V-P-K+

Yoga for Emotional Balance

Sit cross-legged with spine straight. Rest left hand on left knee, with tips of the thumb and index finger touching. Close eyes and block right nostril with right thumb, leaving the rest of the fingers straight up. Inhale deeply through left nostril. When breath is full, extend right pinky over to block left nostril, then release thumb and exhale through right nostril. When breath is completely exhaled, repeat the cycle, inhaling through left nostril only, exhaling through the right. Continue for 11 minutes. Take a few deep breaths and relax.

Please ask your doctor if this exercise is suitable for you.

Happiness is taking things as they are.

Sweet Chai Nutmilk

Takes 10 minutes | makes 500 ml

Ingredients

100 grams hazelnuts (will become 125 grams after soaking),
500 ml hot water, 4 bags of **YOGI TEA® Sweet Chai**,
40 grams of medjool dates (without the pit)

Preparation

Let the hazelnuts soak overnight in water. Strain and rinse the next day. Steep tea in hot water (100°C) for 5 minutes. Remove bags and let it cool. Place nuts and tea in a blender (or hand mixer) and blitz for half a minute until liquid is completely smooth and it turns white. Use cheesecloth to strain the mixture over a bowl. Allow the liquid to drain through the cloth and squeeze the cloth to get all the milk out. Discard the nut fiber left in the cloth. With a hand mixer, mix milk with pitted medjool dates until smooth and creamy.

Tip: *This Sweet Chai YOGI TEA® Nutmilk is used in the Sweet Chai Carrot Pancakes.*

Ayurvedic Info: V-P-K+

Simple Yoga for Longevity

Lie on your back and straighten legs overhead. Hold onto your toes and gently rock on your back. If you can not hold your toes, try the ankles or behind the knees. Synchronise your breath with the movement. Continue for 3 minutes.

Please ask your doctor if this exercise is suitable for you.

Calmness is the highest achievement of the Self.

Oven Roasted Nuts (savory & sweet)

Takes 15 minutes | makes 4 servings each

Ingredients

Savory: 40 grams of cashew nuts, 1 bag of **YOGI TEA®** **Ginseng Flower** (contents), 2 teaspoons avocado oil, 4 pinches of seasalt
Sweet: 40 grams of cashew nuts, 1 bag of **YOGI TEA®** **Bedtime** (contents), 4 teaspoons of maple syrup

Preparation

Savory: Preheat oven to 150°C. In a bowl sprinkle the contents of the YOGI TEA® Ginseng Flower with the cashews and the oil. Mix well and place on a lined baking tray. Place in the oven and roast until they turn golden brown. Add sea salt according to taste.
Sweet: Preheat oven to 150°C. In a bowl sprinkle the contents of the YOGI TEA® Bedtime with the cashews and maple syrup. Mix well and place on a lined baking tray. Place in the oven and roast until they turn golden brown.

Ayurvedic Info: V-P-Ko

Easy Yoga to Aid Digestion

Sit on your heels, keeping your spine straight and your head level. Rest your hands on your knees. Breathe slowly and deeply through the nose for 3–11 minutes. This posture is called Vajrasana or Rock Pose and is an excellent remedy for relieving the negative effects of overeating or eating too quickly. The ancient yogis believed that you could digest rocks when sitting in this posture.

Please ask your doctor if this exercise is suitable for you.

The head must bow before the heart.

Adzuki Choco Spread

Takes 62 – 67 minutes | serves 4

Side dishes

Ingredients

50 grams adzuki beans, 300 ml hot water, 3 bags of
YOGI TEA® Choco, 2 tablespoons of maple syrup, 10 drops of
vanilla essence, pinch of red pepper, pinch of sea salt

Preparation

*Rinse and soak the adzuki beans overnight. Rinse well the next day. Make
tea from water and tea bags. Let steep in hot water (100°C) for 7 – 10 minutes. Cook beans with prepared tea for 50 minutes at very low heat in a
lidded pan. Remove the lid and cook for another 10 minutes to let excess
water evaporate. Turn heat off and allow to cool. Add maple syrup, vanilla,
red pepper and sea salt. Use hand mixer to blend until completely smooth.*

Ayurvedic Info: V-P-K+

Easy Yoga for Strength of Spirit

In ancient times people practiced this exercise to raise their spirits.
Stand with your feet as wide apart as possible without losing your
balance. Keep your arms against your sides and bend the elbows to
form a 90-degree angle, forearms
parallel to the ground, hands and
wrists relaxed. Keeping your
feet in place, rotate your hips in
a large circle for 1 – 3 minutes in
one direction; then reverse the
direction and continue for another
1 – 3 minutes. Relax.

Please ask your doctor if this exercise is suitable for you.

Love is endless trust.

Ginkgo Pumpkin Spread

Takes 65 minutes (+ 45 min. oventime and 15 min. cooling time) | makes 4 small portions

Side dishes

Ingredients

200 grams pumpkin, 50 ml hot water, 2 bags of **YOGI TEA® Ginkgo** plus 3 teaspoons of **YOGI TEA® Ginkgo** (contents), 2 pinches of sea salt, 2 pinches of black pepper

Preparation

Preheat oven to 180°C. Cut pumpkin in even wedges and bake in oven for 45 minutes. Let cool for 15 minutes. Let Ginkgo tea bags steep in hot water (100°C) for 1 hour. In a small pan toast the Gingko tea for 2 minutes. In a blender or with a hand mixer add cooled tea, pumpkin, 3 teaspoons of the roasted Gingko tea, sea salt and black pepper and blend until it forms a smooth spread.

Ayurvedic Info: V-P-K+

Simple Yoga for Energy and Stress Relief

Sit on your heels or on a chair with hands on knees, eyes closed. As you inhale through your nose, arch spine forward, pushing your chest out. Exhale and slump shoulders forward and down, relaxing the spine. Repeat 26 times, keeping a comfortable rhythm.

Please ask your doctor if this exercise is suitable for you.

When you speak to the heart your speech is truthful.

Easy Avocado Spread

Takes 6 minutes | makes 4 portions

Side dishes

Ingredients

140 grams ripe avocado (mashed), 60 grams cucumber
(cut into small cubes), 40 grams sprouted chickpeas,
12 pinches of **YOGI TEA® Stomach Ease** (contents), 4 pinches
of sea salt, 4 pinches of black pepper, 4 squeezes of lemon

Preparation

Place contents from the YOGI TEA® Stomach Ease into a pan and add
pepper, roast spices for 1 minute. Combine cucumber, chickpeas, lemon
juice and sea salt into a bowl and stir well. Add to pan and let simmer for 5
minutes. Serve as a spread or filling or with the Sweet Chai Carrot Pancakes.

Ayurvedic Info: V-P-K+

Yoga Exercise Strengthening Trust

Sit in a comfortable cross-legged sitting position or in a chair with a
straight spine. Raise the arms up over the head with one hand on top
of the other, the palms facing down. If you are male,
place the right palm on top of the left.
If you are female, place the left palm on top of
the right. The thumb tips are together with the
thumbs pointing back. The arms are slightly bent
at the elbows. With the eyes opened very slightly,
look down toward the upper lip and whisper the
mantra „Wa-he Gu-ru".
Duration: 3 minutes.
Please ask your doctor if this exercise is suitable for you.

Inner peace is the essence of life.

Bright Cashew Cream

Takes 5 minutes (+ soaking time overnight) | makes 4 portions

Ingredients

100 grams cashew nuts, 200 ml hot water, 3 bags of **YOGI TEA®**
Bright Mood, 4 pinches of sea salt, generous squeeze of lime juice

Preparation

*Place cashews in a bowl and cover with water and soak overnight. Rinse
and strain cashews. Prepare tea and let steep in hot water (100°C) for 5 minutes. Remove bags and let cool. Use a hand mixer or blends to mix tea and
cashews into a smooth cream. Add sea salt and lime juice. Stir well. Serve.*
Tip: *Serve with Sweet Chai Carrot Pancakes.*

Ayurvedic Info: V-P-K+

Easy Yoga for Energy

Sit cross-legged or on a chair with your spine
straight and feet flat on the floor. Stretch
your arms straight out in front of you,
parallel to the ground, with your palms
facing each other and the fingers wide
apart. Breathe long, deeply and powerfully
through the nose for 1–3 minutes. Then
inhale deeply and, while holding your breath,
make fists of your hands, slowly bringing them to
your chest under maximum tension. Slowly exhale
when your fists touch your chest and relax. Take a few
deep breaths and feel the energy you've created.

Please ask your doctor if this exercise is suitable for you.

Learn to listen to others. Learn to listen to yourself.

Bright Mood Dal Spread

Takes 55 minutes | makes 4 portions

Side dishes

Ingredients

2 teaspoons sesame oil, 1 bag of **YOGI TEA® Bright Mood**
(contents), 100 grams red lentils, 400 ml water, 5 pinches of sea salt,
1 teaspoon sesame oil

Preparation

*Heat sesame oil in a pan. Add the contents from YOGI TEA® tea bag in
sesame oil. Add lentils and stir. Next add water and cover with a lid and
cook for 50 minutes at very low heat. Turn heat off and add 5 pinches of
sea salt and 1 teaspoon of sesame oil. Let the mixture cool and mix until
smooth. Serve with (flat) bread.*

Tip: *If you want it to be less spreadable and more sauce like, you may
choose to add a couple of tablespoons of coconut milk and some extra sea
salt to your liking.*

Ayurvedic Info: V-P-K+

Yoga to Strengthen your Electro-Magnetic Field

Sit in a comfortable position with spine straight. Raise
arms overhead to about 60° (like a big 'Y'). Bring hands
into a half fist, palms facing forward, and extend
thumbs upward. Focus eyes at a point between
the eyebrows. Begin a quick, strong breath
through the nose (pull navel inward while
exhaling, release navel on the inhale). Be
sure to keep your arms straight. Continue
for 1 to 3 minutes. Inhale deeply, hold your
breath for a few moments and enjoy the
positive charge of energy! Exhale and relax.

Please ask your doctor if this exercise is suitable for you.

Don't criticize, and you automatically become intuitive.

Coconut 3 Tea Curry Spread

Takes 5 minutes | makes 250 grams

Ingredients

1 tablespoon of sesame oil, 1 bag of **YOGI TEA® Ginseng** (contents),
1 bag of **YOGI TEA® Classic** (contents), 1 bag of **YOGI TEA® Himalaya**
(contents), 175 ml coconut milk, 1 tablespoon of tomato puree or
organic ketchup, 1 tablespoon of rice syrup, 1 teaspoon of lime juice,
pinch of sea salt, 125 grams tomato (in cubes without seeds)

Preparation

*Toast contents of the YOGI TEA® tea bags in sesame oil until dissolved,
about 1 minute. Add all other ingredients except for the tomatoes. Let
simmer for 3 minutes. Turn heat off and add tomato cubes. Remove from
heat and allow to cool.*

Tip: *Use as a bread spread, side dish or as a spread over steamed or stir
fried vegetables.*

Ayurvedic Info: V-P-Ko

Easy Yoga for Purification

Sit on your heels with your knees spread wide. Bring your forehead
down to the ground and relax in this position with the arms stretched
forward and the palms together. This posture is called Guru Pranam.
Breathe long and deep through the nose for 1–3 minutes. Then slowly
sit up straight, take a few deep breaths and relax. Try this simple pranayam (breathing technique)
coupled with a yogic asana
(posture) for its cleansing
effect.

Please ask your doctor if this exercise is suitable for you.

Count your Blessings.

Echinacea Avocado Cream Sauce

Takes 5 minutes (+ puffing garlic & steeping & cooling tea) | makes 4 portions

Ingredients

140 grams avocado, 2 cloves of "puffed garlic", 100 ml hot water,
2 bags of **YOGI TEA® Echinacea**, 4 pinches of sea salt,
20 drops of lime juice

Preparation

To make "puffed garlic": Place 2 cloves of garlic in the oven with its skin for approximately 30 minutes at 180 °C. Remove from oven and let it cool. Once cooled peel and set aside. Steep YOGI TEA® tea bag in hot water (100 °C) for 3 minutes. Remove bags and allow it to cool. Place avocado, puffed garlic, tea, sea salt and lime juice in blender or use hand mixer. Blend till creamy. Serve.

Tip: *Puff a whole bulb of garlic at the same time. It is most efficient and this way you have puffed garlic readily available all week! You can store it after you let it cool off, in a closed glass jar.*

Ayurvedic Info: VoPoKo

Easy Yoga to Open the Lungs

Stand up straight with your legs slightly apart. Inhale fully while raising your arms up straight over your head and lean back slightly. Exhale fully as you bend forward from the waist, bringing your arms towards the ground and your upper torso towards your legs. This posture is called uttanasana. Continue this smooth movement for 1–3 minutes. Then stand up straight with the arms relaxed by your sides, take a few deep breaths and relax.

Please ask your doctor if this exercise is suitable for you.

Every life needs an anchor.

YOGI TEA®

Ginger Lemon Sesame Crackers

Takes 20 minutes | makes 4 portions

Side dishes

Ingredients

30 grams buckwheat flour, 30 grams sesame seeds, pinch of baking powder, 1 teaspoon of sea salt, 15 grams of salt free tahini, 20 ml water, 2 bags of **YOGI TEA® Ginger Lemon** (contents), pepper

Preparation

Combine all of the ingredients into a bowl. Split mixture into 4 equal size parts. With your hands roll into balls. Place onto baking tray lined with baking paper. Now use palm of hand to make balls into thin discs or squares. Spread a little extra tahini onto each of the crackers. Sprinkle with some fresh ground black pepper and some sea salt, if desired. Bake for 15 minutes in a preheated oven at 180 °C.
Serving tip: *They taste really nice with the Pumpkin Spread.*

Ayurvedic Info: VoPoKo

Easy Yoga to Maintain Health

Sit on your heels and interlace your fingers behind your back. Lower your forehead to the ground in front of your knees and raise the clasped hands up as high as you can, keeping the elbows straight, shoulders pulled away from the ears. Hold this Yoga Mudra posture and breathe long and deeply for 1–3 minutes. Then lower your arms, sit up straight, take a few deep breaths and relax.

Please ask your doctor if this exercise is suitable for you.

Love the spirit. From him you receive the longing of your soul.

Echinacea Lotus Root Chips

Takes 30 minutes (+ soaking time) | makes 4 portions

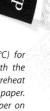

Ingredients

50 grams lotus root, 200 ml hot water, 6 bags of **YOGI TEA® Echinacea**,
6 big pinches of sea salt, some extra sea salt, ground pepper

Preparation

Steep the 6 YOGI TEA® tea bags in 200 ml of hot water (100°C) for 7 minutes. Place lotus root and salt into a bowl and cover with the brewed tea. Allow for it to fully cool, approximately 30 minutes. Preheat oven at 180°C. Strain lotus. Place onto oven tray with baking paper. Sprinkle with some extra sea salt and ground black or pink pepper on top. Bake for approximately 12 minutes until crispy. Turn over half way through for optimal result.

Ayurvedic Info: VoPoKo

Enrich yourself in 2 Minutes

Sit with the legs stretched out in front of you. Come into Yoga Mudra by interlacing the fingers behind the back, keeping the elbows straight. Inhale in 4 parts as you bend forward from your hips, raising your arms up as high as possible, stretching them away from the shoulders. Exhale in one breath as you return upright. Continue rhythmically coordinating the movement with the breath for 2 minutes. This exercise promotes endurance.

Please ask your doctor if this exercise is suitable for you.

Joy is the essence of success.

Bedtime Sweet Potato Bread

Takes 55 minutes | makes 1 whole bread

Ingredients

Solids: 300 grams brown rice flour, 150 grams almond flour,
36 grams baking powder, 1 teaspoon sea salt (9 large pinches),
3 bags of **YOGI TEA® Bedtime**
Fluids: 480 grams sweet potato (roasted) in skin, 3 tablespoons
white almond butter, 6 tablespoons of water (or almond milk),
3 tablespoons flaxseeds, 9 tablespoons of water

Preparation

Roast the sweet potato in their skin for approximately 30 – 40 minutes (depending on their size) in a preheated oven at 180 °C. Let cool. Remove their skins and mash using a fork. Combine all solids in a large bowl. Combine sweet potato mash with almond butter and 6 tablespoons of water (or almond milk). Place whole flaxseeds in grinder and bruise. Add water and bruise more until the mixture becomes slimy. Add to the sweet potato mash mixture. Add to the solids. Combine well using a wooden spoon and your hands. Line the cake tin with baking paper and add dough. Sprinkle with some whole flaxseeds. Bake for 25 to 30 minutes in a preheated oven at 180 °C. Let cool. Slice.

Ayurvedic Info: VoPoKo

Yoga for Balance

Sit up straight, cross-legged or in a chair with your feet on the floor. Bending your right elbow, raise the right hand to ear level as if taking an oath, with the palm facing forward, the middle and index fingers pointing up and the thumb locking the other 2 fingers down. The fingers of the left hand are in the same position, but with the two straight fingers touching the center of the chest. Close your eyes and breathe long and deep through the nose. Imagine the breath flowing from the nose to the center of the forehead, then down to the heart. Continue for 3–11 minutes, then relax.

Please ask your doctor if this exercise is suitable for you.

Take a minute every day to be you.

Throat Comfort Sweet Bread

Takes 30 minutes | makes 1 whole bread

Ingredients

Dry ingredients: 100 grams whole rice flour, 60 grams coconut blossom sugar, 50 grams chestnut flour, 40 grams arrow root, ½ teaspoon of baking powder, ½ teaspoon of fine sea salt, 12 bags of **YOGI TEA®** **Throat Comfort** (contents), 12 grams fresh thyme (finely chopped)

Wet ingredients: 240 grams ripe banana, 60 grams fresh ginger (peeled), 20 grams coconut oil

Preparation

Mix all dry ingredients into a bowl. In a separate bowl mash the banana, and grate ginger, combine together and add coconut oil. Combine wet and dry ingredients. Mix well. Place into muffin tins or small 1 serving size cake forms. Bake in preheated oven at 180 °C for 25 minutes. Let cool.

Tip: *Tastes great with banana cream. To make this, use a hand mixer or blender to blitz bananas and a few drops of lime juice into a smooth and creamy 'butter'.*

Ayurvedic Info: VoPoKo

Easy Yoga to Bring Energy to the Throat

Sit cross-legged or on a chair with your spine straight and feet flat on the floor. Rest your hands on your knees with your eyes closed. Inhale through the nose as you turn your head so you are facing over your left shoulder; exhale through the nose as you turn your head so you are facing over the right shoulder. Continue for 1–3 minutes. Then facing straight ahead, take a few deep breaths and relax. Feel your throat fill with energy, warmth and light!

Please ask your doctor if this exercise is suitable for you.

Meditation carries you through times of difficulties.

Ginkgo Walnut Pesto Sauce

Takes 5 minutes | makes 60 grams = 4 small portions

Ingredients

25 grams walnuts, 50 ml hot water, 1 bag of **YOGI TEA® Ginkgo**,
2 grams purslane (or another green leafy vegetable),
2 grams rocket salad, 3 pinches of sea salt, 8 drops of lemon juice

Preparation

*Steep one YOGI TEA® Ginkgo tea bag in hot water (100 °C) for 5 minutes.
Remove bag and allow to cool. Place the walnuts, tea, purslane, rocket
salad, sea salt and lemon juice in a blender or in a bowl if you use a hand
mixer. Mix until creamy. Place in a lidded glass jar and store in the fridge.
This sauce keeps for 4 – 5 days.*

Ayurvedic Info: V-P-K+

Yoga Exercise for Strength and Endurance

Sit with spine straight and place your
hands on your knees. Keep the elbows
straight. Inhale deep and hold your
breath. Start flexing your spine back
and forth until you cannot hold your
breath any longer.
Exhale. Inhale and start again.
Time: 3 – 11 Minutes.

Please ask your doctor if this exercise
is suitable for you.

Your intuition knows all.

Licorice Pineapple Relish

Takes 10 minutes | makes 140 grams = 4 portions as a side dish

Ingredients

150 grams pineapple (cut into small even sized cubes)
60 grams cucumber (cut into small even sized cubes), ½ teaspoon
fresh red chili (finely chopped), 1 tablespoon coconut oil,
5 pinches of **YOGI TEA® Licorice** (contents), 2 pinches of sea salt

Preparation

*Heat oil in a pan. When oil is hot add 5 pinches of YOGI TEA® Licorice tea
contents and chopped chili. Let roast for half a minute. Add pineapple
and cucumber. Let the mixture simmer all the way through approximately
5 minutes, stirring occasionally. Turn heat off and let cool. Add sea salt, stir
and serve.*

Ayurvedic Info: VoP+K-

Simple Yoga for Awareness

Sit with your legs crossed. Stretch your arms out to the sides, parallel
to the ground and with your fists clenched into tight lion's paws.
Cross your wrists over your head and return your arms to your sides,
alternating right over left,
then left over right. Move
powerfully and rhyth-
mically for 3 minutes
with powerful breath.
Then stretch out your
tongue all the way and
continue for another minute.
Relax.

Please ask your doctor if this exercise
is suitable for you.

Without meditation, the mind will not be a partner.

Sweet Chili Mango Sauce

Takes 5 minutes (+ tea steeping time) | makes 200 ml / 4 portions

Ingredients

75 ml hot water, 2 bags of **YOGI TEA® Sweet Chili**, 125 grams of
ripe mango (without peel), 2 – 4 pinches of fresh red chili

Preparation

Brew tea in hot water (100 °C) for a couple of hours. Remove bags, add chopped mango and chopped red chili. In a blender or in a bowl with a hand mixer blend until smooth. Store in fridge in airtight glass jar. Use within 3 days.

Ayurvedic Info: V-P+K-

Yoga for Purification

Hold hands under your knees and
roll onto back keeping the knees
straight. Then roll forward bringing
your head to your knees. Continue
for 2 minutes. Relax.
Please ask your doctor if this
exercise is suitable for you.

The blossoms of spring tell the story from open hearts.

Women's Chutney

Takes 37 minutes | makes 4 portions

Ingredients

250 grams beetroot (peeled and cut into small cubes),
70 grams medjool dates (without the pit), 30 grams raisins,
6 cardamom pods, 6 cloves, 6 pepper corns, 200 ml hot water,
4 bags of **YOGI TEA® Women's Balance**

Preparation

Steep 4 bags YOGI TEA® Women's Balance in 200 ml hot water (100 °C) for 7 minutes. Remove tea bags. Place beetroot, medjool dates, raisins, cardamom, cloves, pepper corns and tea in a pan. Cover with lid and cook on a very low fire for about 30 minutes. Check every now and then to see if there is still liquid in the pan. Turn off heat and let cool. Serve.

Ayurvedic Info: V-PoK-

Breathing for Endurance

Sit crosslegged or in a chair, spine straight. Wrap your hands around your knees, with your arms straight. Inhale and hold your breath. Flex your spine back and forth as long as you can hold it before you need to exhale. Inhale again, hold and continue this exercise for 3 minutes.

Please ask your doctor if this exercise is suitable for you.

Feel good, do good, be good.

Green Energy Dressing

Takes 2 minutes (+ tea steeping time) | makes 150 ml

Ingredients

150 ml hot water, 2 bags of **YOGI TEA® Green Energy**,
6 tablespoons of rice syrup, 3 tablespoons of sunflower oil,
1½ cm vanilla pod (scrapings)

Preparation

Steep 2 bags of YOGI TEA® Green Energy for 1 hour in 150 ml of hot water (100°C). Add rice syrup and vanilla scraping. Mix on low with a hand mixer or blender and slowly add oil. Store in airtight glass jar and use when desired.

Ayurvedic Info: V-PoKo

Yoga for Energy

Stand comfortably and straight with feet slightly apart. Stretch your arms high above your head, preferably touching your ears, and your hands clasped. Inhale through your nose. Keeping your arms stretched up high, hunker down into a squat (crow pose) on the exhale, with your feet firmly on the ground and balanced. Instantly on the inhale come back up to standing with a straight spine and your head upright and facing forward. Breathing strongly through your nose, continue this exercise for 3 minutes and enjoy the new energy that you may gain.

Please ask your doctor if this exercise is suitable for you.

Gratefulness is the door to abundance.

Detox Date Dressing

Takes 5 – 10 minutes | makes 155 ml

Ingredients

50 ml grapefruit juice (juice from 1 small grapefruit),
75 ml hot water, 2 bags of **YOGI TEA® Detox**, 30 grams
medjool dates (without the pit), 1 tablespoon flaxseed oil,
5 large fresh mint leaves

Preparation

Steep the YOGI TEA® tea bags in hot water (100 °C) for 5 minutes. Remove the tea bags, let tea cool. Add grapefruit juice, dates, mint leaves to a blender and blend on low while slowly adding the flaxseed oil. Store in the fridge in a closed glass flask and use when desired.

Ayurvedic Info: VoPoK-

Breath of Fire

Breath of fire is a strong, quick breath done from the navel point. Consciously pull in the navel while exhaling through the nose, inhaling will happen automaticaly by relaxing the belly. Slowly increase the pace until breathing 2 – 3 times per second in and out through the nose. Continue for 1 – 3 minutes. Breath of fire energises and ignites the fire of life.

Please ask your doctor if this exercise is suitable for you.

Love is without pain. It is in bloom. It is blessed.

Women's Energy Raspberry Dressing

Takes 6 minutes | makes 150 ml

Ingredients

100 ml hot water, 2 bags of **YOGI TEA® Women's Energy**,
40 grams raspberries, 2 teaspoons rice syrup, 1 teaspoon olive oil,
¼ teaspoon lime zest, juice of a ½ lime, 2 pinches of sea salt

Preparation

*Let YOGI TEA® tea bags steep in hot water (100 °C) for 5 minutes. Remove
and let cool. Add all ingredients, except for olive oil into a blender or a bowl
if using a hand mixer. Blend slowly, while blending, drizzle in the olive oil
until it becomes one homogenous fluid.*

Ayurvedic Info: V-PoKo

Yoga for Energy – Archer Pose

Stand comfortably with your right leg forward and your left leg turned out,
keeping the body square. Bend the right knee and let your right leg carry
your weight. Now make your right hand into a fist with the thumb pointing
upwards, stretching the right arm straight out so that the thumbnail is held
at eye level. Imagine that you are holding an bow with your right hand, the
bow string is pulled back with
your left hand and arm. Breathe
slowly and deeply whilst
concentrating on your
imaginary target. Hold the
posture for 1–3 minutes each
side. (Archer Pose is believed to
strengthen and balance the
nervous system.)
Please ask your doctor if this
exercise is suitable for you.

It is your birthright to be happy.

Forever Young Miso Dressing

Takes 7 minutes | makes approximately 150 ml = 4 portions

Ingredients

150 ml hot water, 4 bags of **YOGI TEA® Forever Young**,
3 large teaspoons of white miso paste, 3 teaspoons of rice syrup,
3 teaspoons of maple syrup, 15 leaves of fresh sage,
3 pinches of sea salt

Preparation

*Steep YOGI TEA® tea bags in hot water (100 °C) for 5 minutes. Remove bags
and let it cool. Add miso paste, rice syrup, maple syrup, sage and salt and
use hand mixer or blender to make it into a creamy dressing.*

Ayurvedic Info: VoPoK-

Easy Yogic Breathing for a Restful Sleep

Before bed, a great way to relax is to
practice long, slow, deep breathing. Sit
in a comfortable cross-legged position,
with your spine straight and shoulders
relaxed. Rest your hands in your lap
with palms facing up. Close your eyes
and completely relax. Breathe through
the nose slowly and deeply. Stay focused on
your breath as it fills your lungs, expanding the
diaphragm. Exhale and empty the lungs completely.
Continue for 1–5 minutes. Then lie down on your
right side and enjoy a deep and restful sleep.
Please ask your doctor if this exercise is suitable for you.

Make today better than yesterday.

Bright Mood Mustard Dressing

Takes 7 minutes | makes 150 ml

Ingredients

100 ml hot water, 4 bags of **YOGI TEA® Bright Mood**,
1 small teaspoon of mustard, 2 big teaspoons of rice syrup,
juice of a ½ lime, 2 pinches of sea salt, 2 pinches of black pepper

Preparation

Let the YOGI TEA® tea bags steep in hot water (100°C) for 5 minutes.
Remove bags and let cool. Add mustard, rice syrup, lime juice, salt and
pepper and use hand mixer or blender to blitz into a creamy dressing.

Ayurvedic Info: V-PoKo

Yoga to bring peace of mind

A steady rhythm creates a steady mind. Sit cross-legged or in a chair
with feet flat. With eyes gently closed, close off right nostril with
right hand and take smooth, equal
breaths through the left nostril.
Your target breath rate is 4 to 6
breaths per minute. Then, switch
sides. Feeling at peace starts with
breathing deep.

Please ask your doctor if this exercise is suitable for you.

All we love deeply becomes part of us.

Rose Pistachio Rice

Takes 45 minutes | serves 1

Main dishes

Ingredients

200 grams brown (basmati) rice, 200 ml hot water, 4 bags of
YOGI TEA® Rose, 40 unsalted pistachio nuts (without shell),
8 pinches of cardamom powder, 8 pinches of dried rose petals,
8 pinches of sea salt, 8 pinches of lemon or lime zest

Preparation

*Place rice and water in pan, cover with lid. Cook rice on a low heat for 40
minutes, or given cooking time. Add contents of 4 bags of YOGI TEA® Rose
for last 4 minutes of cooking time. Turn heat off, add pistachios, cardamom
powder, rose petals and sea salt. Let cool. Grate some fresh lemon or lime
zest on top. Serve.*

Ayurvedic Info: V-P-K+

Yoga for Joy and Spirit

Sit cross-legged with your spine straight folding
your hands behind your back. Raise your arms
stretching the hands away from your body.
Inhaling swing the arms to the right, exhaling
to the left. Move arms and upper body as a
unit. Continue for 3 minutes with quick and
powerful movements. Inhale deeply, hold
your breath briefly, then relax.

Please ask your doctor if this exercise is suitable
for you.

Being deeply loved by someone gives you strength.

Breathe Deep Soup

Takes 10 minutes | makes 4 large portions

Ingredients

900 grams zucchini, 200 grams green peas, 1 tablespoon extra virgin coconut oil, 3 – 4 bags of **YOGI TEA® Breathe Deep** (content), sea salt to taste

Preparation

Cook zucchini and green peas, covered by water in a lidded pan until soft, approximately 10 minutes. Add the contents of the YOGI TEA® Breathe Deep bags one minute before time. Let cook for a minute or so, then turn off the heat. Add coconut oil and blend using a handmixer or blender. Add seasalt to taste. Enjoy!

Ayurvedic Info: V-P-Ko

Yoga to make you strong

Sit crosslegged with hands on your knees, keeping your arms straight. Inhale and hold your breath. Flex your spine back and forth as many times as you can before you have to exhale. Inhale and repeat. Continue for 3-4 minutes. Then relax and enjoy.

Please ask your doctor if this exercise is suitable for you.

Don't get lost in the small-talk of the every day.

Rootsy Classic Stew

Takes 35 minutes | serves 2 – 4

Ingredients

200 grams sliced carrot (cut into discs), 225 grams chestnuts
(precooked), 350 grams white cabbage (sliced in strips),
375 grams sweet potato (cubed), 1 teaspoon sesame oil,
2 bags of **YOGI TEA® Classic** (content), 2 teaspoons fenugreek,
1 teaspoon tamari, few pinches of sea salt, ½ cup water

Preparation

*Heat oil in large skillet. Add fenugreek. When fenugreek pops add content
of YOGI TEA® Classic tea bags. Add carrot, cabbage and sweet potato.
Add water. Place lid on pan and let stew at medium heat for approximately
20 minutes check the contents every now and than and add a bit of extra
water to prevent vegetables from sticking to the bottom of the pan. Shake
the pan. After 20 minutes of stewing add chestnuts, half a cup of water,
1 teaspoon of tamari and a few pinches of sea salt. Let stew for another
10 minutes and serve.*

Ayurvedic Info: V-P-Ko

Self-confidence (Affirmation)

Sometimes we find ouselves dependent on appraisal
and acceptance from others. There
is a simple affirmation which brings
back our own strength: Press your
thumb on the mount below the
pinky and close the hand in a fist.
Say to yourself before you meet
somebody: "I am healthy, I am
happy, I am great".

Please ask your doctor if this exercise
is suitable for you.

Find out what is within each heart.

Classic Eggplant

Takes 15 minutes | makes 4 portions

Ingredients

275 grams eggplant (small cubes), 215 grams tomato (wedges),
150 grams oyster mushrooms, 75 grams shiitake, 1 large onion
(rings), 3 tablespoons of tamari, 1 tablespoon of coconut oil,
2 bags of **YOGI TEA® Classic** (contents), fresh coriander (optional)

Preparation

*Heat coconut oil in large skillet. Add content from 2 YOGI TEA® Classic tea
bags. Roast for half a minute. Add onion. Fry until slightly glazed then add
1 tablespoon of tamari. Add eggplant cubes and mushrooms. Stir and add
another tablespoon of tamari. Wait until the eggplant is slightly soft. Then
stir in tomato and another tablespoon of tamari. Fry for a 3 – 5 minutes longer until eggplant is soft, mushrooms are well cooked and tomato is still
firm yet warm.*
Tip: *Serve, for example sprinkled with fresh coriander and alongside rice
or Spice Crusted Carrots.*

Ayurvedic Info: V-P-K+

Easy Yoga for Stronger Resistance

Sit on your heels and interlock your fingers behind your head, palms
on your neck. Inhale deeply, then exhale and slowly bring your
forehead to the floor. Try to keep your spine straight. Inhale again as
you slowly come up. Continue the motion for 1–3 minutes, breathing
powerfully through the nose.
Then sit up straight, take a few
deep breaths and relax. The
practice of yoga balances the
glandular system, strengthens
the nervous system and enables
us to harness and balance the
energy of the mind.

Please ask your doctor if this
exercise is suitable for you.

Give up your resistance to change.

Calming Kitcheree

Takes 65 minutes | makes 4 portions

Ingredients

200 grams brown rice, 100 grams red lentils, 4 pinches
cumin seeds, 4 pinches mustard seeds, 4 pinches fenugreek seeds,
1 tablespoon sesame oil, 1200 ml water, strips of kombu,
8 bags of **YOGI TEA® Calming** (contents)

Preparation

*Place sesame oil in a large pan, heat and add the seeds. Fry until they start
to be fragrant and pop. Add rice, lentils, water and kombu. Bring to a boil
and cook to a low heat for 60 minutes, covered by a lid. Add the contents of
the 8 tea bags during the last 5 minutes of cooking. Turn heat off.*
Tip: *Tastes great with the Rootsy Classic Stew or the Spice Crusted Carrots.*

Ayurvedic Info: V-P-Ko

Breathing for Relaxation

Sit crosslegged or in a chair with
a straight spine. Close your right
nostril with your right thumb and
breathe through your left nostril.
Duration: 3 minutes.

Please ask your doctor if this exercise is
suitable for you.

Laughter is a melody, a concert from the heart.

Sweet Chai Carrot Pancakes

Takes 5 minutes | makes 4 pancakes

Ingredients

100 grams of finely grated carrot, 160 grams of buckwheat flour,
480 ml **YOGI TEA® Sweet Chai** Nutmilk (see recipe on page 17),
60 grams of raisins, 4 pinches of sea salt, 4 teaspoons of coconut oil

Preparation

*Combine flour, Sweet Chai Nutmilk, raisins, and sea salt in a bowl. Stir well.
The batter should be thick. Heat coconut oil in a pan or in a skillet to medium high heat. Add one fourth of the batter. These pancakes are meant to be
thick, so add the batter in a thick layer. Cook for a few minutes on one side.
Flip. Cook a few minutes on the second side until golden.*
Tip: *Tastes lovely with the Bright Cashew Cream or Easy Avocado Spread.*

Ayurvedic Info: V-P-K+

Breath to Balance the Mind's Mental Energy

Sit cross-legged with your spine straight. Arms are straight with the
sides of the hands resting on the knees. The tips of the forefingers and
thumbs are together creating a circle,
and the other fingers are straight.
The eyes are open and gazing straight
ahead. Inhale through the nose for
5 seconds. Hold the breath for 10 seconds
and then exhale through the nose for 5 seconds.
Continue for 3–11 minutes. Focus on the inflow
and outflow of the breath.

Please ask your doctor if this exercise is suitable for you.

Patience is the key of joy.

Red Heartwarming Soup

Takes 15 minutes | makes 4 portions (as starters)

Ingredients

200 grams of tomato, 300 grams of red bell pepper,
60 grams of coconut milk, sea salt to taste,
1 bag of **YOGI TEA® Heartwarming** (contents)

Preparation

Place tomato and pepper in a pan with ample amount of water, yet not covering the vegetables. Cook with the lid on for 8 minutes. Add contents of the tea bag and cook for another 2 minutes. Turn the heat off, add coconut milk. Use hand mixer or blender to make into a smooth creamy soup. Add sea salt to taste. Serve.

Ayurvedic Info: V-P-K+

Yoga Position for Blessings (Gurprasad)

Sit in a comfortable sitting position, upper arms pressed against rib cage, elbows bent so that hands are at heart level. Cup the hands together, palms facing up. Breathe long and deep. Allow yourself to relax and receive blessings.
Continue for 3 – 31 minutes.

Please ask your doctor if this exercise is suitable for you.

Speak simply, straight and with a smile.

Sweet Chili Popcorn Soup

Takes 20 minutes | makes 4 portions

Ingredients

Spiced oil: 6 tablespoons of sunflower oil, 4 bags of
YOGI TEA® Sweet Chili (contents), 2 cm of fresh red chili
Soup: 460 grams corn (readily useable / precooked),
2 teaspoons of sea salt (or to taste), fresh red chili

Preparation

To make spiced oil: Heat the contents of the tea bags plus the fresh chili in a
pan with sunflower oil and simmer on very low fire for 10 minutes or so. Turn
heat off and let sit until fully cooled. Run through fine sieve. Set oil aside.
Soup: Place fresh corn kernels in a pan with ample amounts of water. Make
sure the corn is fully covered. Cook for 5 minutes. Turn heat off and use hand
mixer to blend into a creamy soup. You might have to add a bit more water to
make the right consistency. Add sea salt and 3 tablespoons of spice oil. Blend
again until to combine and make extra smooth. For an extra silky cream
consistency pass through a sieve. Place soup in bowl, drizzle with some extra
spice oil, fresh chili and serve.

Ayurvedic Info: V-P+K-

Breath to Balance the Mind's Mental Energy

Sit cross-legged with your spine straight. Arms are straight with the
sides of the hands resting on the knees. The tips of the forefingers and
thumbs are together creating a circle,
and the other fingers are straight.
The eyes are open and gazing
straight ahead. Inhale through the
nose for 5 seconds. Hold the breath
for 10 seconds and then exhale
through the nose for 5 seconds. Continue
for 3 – 11 minutes. Focus on the inflow and
outflow of the breath.

Please ask your doctor if this exercise is suitable for you.

Recognize the other person is you.

Ginger Lemon Broccoli Stir-Fry

Takes 15 minutes (+ tea steeping time) | makes 4 portions

Ingredients

2 large onions (in rings), large broccoli head, 2 medium zucchinis (cut into thin slices), ⅔ of cucumber (julienned), 100 ml hot water, 2 bags of **YOGI TEA® Ginger Lemon**, 6 teaspoons of tamari, 2 teaspoons of coconut oil, 2 bags of **YOGI TEA® Ginger Lemon** (contents)

Preparation

Make tea with 100 ml hot water (100 °C) and 2 YOGI TEA® tea bags. Steep for at least 30 minutes. Remove bags. Heat coconut oil in skillet. Warm content of 2 YOGI TEA® Ginger Lemon in oil. Add onion. Fry until clear. Cut broccoli in even pieces. Use both stalks as well as florets. Add to pan and stir-fry for few minutes. Add 2 teaspoons of tamari. Stir. Add a big splash of cooled tea. Let fry for a few minutes. Add zucchini. Add 2 teaspoons of tamari and a big splash of tea. Add cucumber. Stir and fry for a few minutes. Add last two teaspoons of tamari and a big splash of tea. Turn heat off after a minute or so. Serve with brown rice or any other desired grain.

Ayurvedic Info: V-P-K+

Simple Yoga for Vitality

Lying on your back, kick alternately with your left and right heels against your buttocks, always keeping the alternate leg straight. Inhale as one heel kicks, exhale as the other kicks. Continue for 1–3 minutes.

Please ask your doctor if this exercise is suitable for you.

When in doubt, do the courageous thing.

Roasted Cauliflower
with Peanut Rooibush Dressing

Takes 60 minutes | serves 4

Ingredients

1 head of cauliflower (a 950 grams), 100 ml hot water, 1 bag of
YOGI TEA® Rooibos, 75 grams peanut butter, 1 tablespoon lemon juice,
1 tablespoon tamari, 5 grams coconut cream, 2 small handfuls of
peanuts (roughly chopped), big bunch of fresh coriander

Preparation

*Put whole cauliflower in a pan into a preheated oven. Bake for 60 minutes
at 180 °C. Make tea from 100 ml hot water (100 °C) and 1 bag of YOGI TEA®
Rooibos. Let steep for 7 minutes, remove tea bag. To make dressing using a
hand mixer blend peanut butter, warm tea, lemon juice, tamari and coconut cream. Cut the roasted cauliflower in florets. Cut the florets in equally
thin slices. Place them onto a large plate and drizzle with sauce. Add freshly
chopped coriander and chopped peanuts. Mix and serve.*

Ayurvedic Info: V-P-K+

Simple Yoga for Renewal

Hold ring and small fingers with thumb, index and middle fingers
straight. Arms are straight and parallel from floor, out to the sides with
palms forward. Pull shoulders
down and neck straight. Begin
circling the arms in small circles
backwards. Breath is relaxed but
deep. Continue for 1 – 3 minutes
with the eyes closed.

Please ask your doctor if this exercise
is suitable for you.

Everything and everyone is bound together.

Bright Mood Millet Sushi

Takes 45 minutes | makes 4 rolls

Ingredients

4 sheets of nori, 100 grams millet, 2 cardamom pods, 1 bag of
YOGI TEA® Bright Mood (contents), 4 teaspoons apple cider vinegar,
4 teaspoons rice syrup, 100 grams ripe avocado (mashed), 60 gram
cucumber (thin strips), 20 grams (leek) sprouts, 80 grams avocado (thin strips)

Preparation

Cook millet in a covered pan on low heat for 13 minutes in twice as much water. Add the contents of the bag of YOGI TEA® Bright Mood during the last 3 minutes of cooking. Turn the heat off, add apple cider vinegar and rice syrup and let cool. Add 100 grams of mashed avocado and stir really well. Place sheet of nori on sushi rolling mat. Place one fourth of the millet mixture on the lower part of the sheet, from the middle down. Make sure the millet covers the whole of the lower part except 1 centimeter at the bottom. Place the cucumber strips in one long line horizontally, halfway on the millet. Place avocado strips on top of millet. Place sprouts on top of avocado. Now grab the bottom of the sheet and rolling mat. Use finger to hold the cucumber, avocado and sprouts in place. Roll bottom part of sheet over to the top of the millet patch. Press and roll until a beautiful maki sushi roll appears. Use your finger and a little tamari to wet the edge of the nori sheet and make it stick together. Cut into 5 – 6 equal pieces using a very sharp knife. Serve with some extra tamari.

Ayurvedic Info: V-P-K+

Simple Yoga to Renew and Rejuvenate

Lie on your back, press your knees to
your chest and hold tightly with your
arms and hands. Raise your head and
bring your nose between the knees.
Breathe with a rapid breath through
the nose, pulling your navel in with
the exhale and pushing out with the
inhale. Continue for 1 minute. Relax
on back.

Please ask your doctor if this exercise is suitable
for you.

Let life be with you, not against you.

Calming Corn Cakes

Takes 15 minutes | makes 4 cakes

Main dishes

Ingredients

230 grams corn kernels, 4 tablespoons of rice flour, 1 tablespoon of avocado oil (or sunflower), 25 grams onion (finely chopped), 10 grams celery (finely chopped), 2 to 3 bags of **YOGI TEA® Calming** (contents), 2 large pinches of sea salt, 2 tablespoons extra rice flour for dusting, 4 teaspoons sesame oil for frying

Preparation

Remove and strain corn kernels from the glass jar, and place into bowl. Add rice flour, avocado oil, onion, celery, contents of the YOGI TEA® tea bags and sea salt. Use hand mixer to mash this mixture until almost all of the corn kernels are a puree. Use hands to form a nice dough. Divide into four and make this into even sized balls. Use hands to make these balls into discs. Dust with extra rice flour to make sure they are not too wet and sticky. Put sesame oil in the skillet, heat and add corn cakes. Fry until golden, flip over and fry the other side. Take out of the pan. Let cool slightly. Serve.

Ayurvedic Info: VoP-Ko

Breathing for being Calm and Conscious

Sit crosslegged or in a chair with a straight spine. Your hands are on your knees, with your arms straight. Breathe long and deep and consciously. Understand the life force which your breath is for your being. Duration: 3 minutes.

Please ask your doctor if this exercise is suitable for you.

There is no way to happiness – happiness is the way.

Calming Chickpea Wrap

Takes 10 minutes | makes 4

Ingredients

100 grams chickpea flour, 40 grams buckwheat flour,
4 bags of **YOGI TEA® Calming** (contents), 4 big pinches of sea salt,
280 ml water, 4 teaspoons of sesame oil

Preparation

Combine flour, YOGI TEA® Calming contents and sea salt into a bowl. Slowly
add water until it thickens into pancake batter. Heat sesame oil in skillet.
Add one fourth of batter and cook on each side until light golden brown.
Repeat.
Tip: Tastes great with a spread and green salad or veggie filling.

Ayurvedic Info: V-PoKo

Easy Yogic Breathing to Relax

Sit in a cross-legged position or on a chair with your spine straight and
feet flat on the floor. Block off your right nostril with your right index
finger and breathe deeply and slowly
through the left nostril. Let your
left hand relax in your lap. Eyes are
closed. Continue for 1–5 minutes.
Practice this pranayam to realise the
calming and receptive side of your
being.

Please ask your doctor if this exercise is
suitable for you.

Wake up to your own capacity of real love.

Beetroot Coconut Soup

Takes 10 minutes | makes 4 portions

Ingredients

1120 grams beetroot, 400 ml coconut milk, 4 teaspoons coconut oil,
8 pinches of dried lemon grass powder, 4 pieces of star anise,
4 cm fresh red peppers, 2 bags of **YOGI TEA® Forever Young** (contents),
2 teaspoon (= 8 grams) of sea salt

Preparation

Juice the beetroot. This amount will become 400 ml of juice. Mix juice and
coconut milk. Heat coconut oil in skillet. Add lemon grass powder. Fry for
a minute or so. Add beetroot juice and coconut milk. Cut red peppers into
small strips. Add star anise and red peppers to soup. Place on medium low
heat for 7 minutes or so. Add contents of YOGI TEA® bags 4 minutes before
you turn the heat off. Season with sea salt.

Tip: Use the pulp that's left over after the juicing to make the Beetroot
Muesli Crunch.

Ayurvedic Info: V-PoKo

Yoga for Serenity

Sit cross-legged or in a chair with
spine straight and feet flat. Now,
close your eyes and block right
nostril with right hand. Take deep,
slow breaths through the left
nostril. Continue for 1 to 3 minutes. Let the positive and relaxing
energy take over.

Please ask your doctor if this exercise is
suitable for you.

Be aware of the thoughts you are thinking.

Heartwarming Spinach Dosas

Takes 10 minutes (+ fermentation time) | makes 4

Ingredients

50 grams whole spelt flour, 100 ml water (room temperature),
2 teaspoons spinach juice, ½ bag of **YOGI TEA® Heartwarming**
(contents), 2 pinches of sea salt

Preparation

*Combine the flour and the water in a bowl and cover with a clean towel.
Let ferment at room temperature for 6 hours. Add spinach juice, contents of
½ tea bag and sea salt. Stir. Heat a 'non stick' skillet on high heat. When it's
hot add a really thin layer of batter, using a spatula to make it even thinner.
Cook until dosa turns over easily, after a minute or so. Flip and cook side
two. Serve, with Bright Mood Dal Spread.*

Tip: *The fermentation is optional. If you don't have that much time you
may choose to combine the ingredients and cook immediately.*

Ayurvedic Info: V-P-Ko

Relax in 2 Minutes

Sit cross-legged. Stretch the arms out straight and stiff in
front of you, hands in fists, with the palm sides facing
down. At the level of your heart center, begin rotating
the fists in small circles, the right fist clockwise
and the left fist counter clockwise. Keep the elbows straight and fists tight. Move the shoulder
blades and the muscles underneath the shoulder area. Continue powerfully for 2 minutes
with a long deep breath through the nose.

Please ask your doctor if this exercise is suitable for
you.

Hope for the best, but be prepared for the worst.

Himalayan Buckwheat Wraps

Takes 14 minutes | makes 4

Ingredients

200 grams buckwheat flour, 400 ml hot water,
8 bags of **YOGI TEA® Himalaya**, 8 pinches of nigella
(black cumin), 4 teaspoons of coconut oil

Preparation

Let the YOGI TEA® tea bags steep in hot water (100 °C) for at least 10 minutes.
Remove tea bags. Add flour to tea in a bowl and mix well using whisk. Heat
oil in skillet. Add pinch of nigella (black cumin) to pan. Add ¼ of batter.
Sprinkle top with another pinch of nigella. Let cook for a few minutes, flip
over and let cook for another few minutes.

Ayurvedic Info: V-P-Ko

Simple Yoga for Stamina

Sit with your legs crossed and interlace
your fingers. Bring your hands above your
head and hold them there. Keep your eyes
1/10 open. Inhale long and deep and hold,
then exhale and hold. Continue with very
long and deep breaths for 3 – 4 minutes.

Please ask your doctor if this exercise is
suitable for you.

It always looks impossible until it's done.

Men's Veggie Protein Bowl

Takes 20 minutes | makes 4 portions

Main dishes

Ingredients

800 ml water, 2 red onions (cut into discs), 2 tablespoons of tamari,
2 tablespoons genmai miso, 2 strips of kombu, 160 grams shiitake,
80 grams red cabbage, 80 grams frozen green peas (defrosted),
80 grams zucchini, 2 bags of **YOGI TEA® Men's tea** (contents)

Preparation

*Place water, onion, tamari, miso, kombu and shiitake into a large soup
pan. Bring to boil, cover with lid and turn the heat to low. After 10 minutes
add red cabbage. Place lid back on and cook for 4 more minutes. Then add
strips of zucchini, defrosted green peas and the contents of the YOGI TEA®
tea bags. Let simmer for 5 more minutes. Switch heat off. Serve.*

Ayurvedic Info: V-PoKo

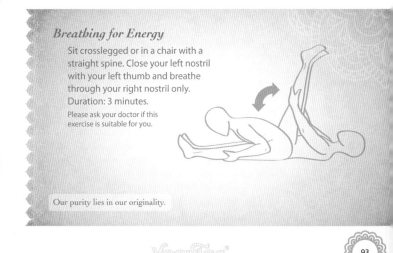

Breathing for Energy

Sit crosslegged or in a chair with a
straight spine. Close your left nostril
with your left thumb and breathe
through your right nostril only.
Duration: 3 minutes.

Please ask your doctor if this
exercise is suitable for you.

Our purity lies in our originality.

Spice Crusted Carrots

Takes 5 minutes (+ 60 minutes oven time) | makes 4 portions

Ingredients

700 grams thin carrots, 3 bags of **YOGI TEA® Stomach Ease** (contents), 4 tablespoons of sesame oil, 4 pinches of sea salt

Preparation

Combine contents of the 3 bags of YOGI TEA® Stomach Ease with sesame oil and sea salt. Rub carrots with this mixture. Make sure all carrots are fully covered. Preheat oven to 180°C and roast carrots for 60 minutes. Let cool. Serve.

Ayurvedic Info: V-P-Ko

Yoga to Uplift your Spirit

Sit cross-legged or in a chair with spine straight and feet flat. With eyes gently closed, inhale through the nose in four even sniffs and exhale in one long breath. Use your complete lung capacity and keep breaths smooth. Sit back, smile and enjoy some bliss.

Please ask your doctor if this exercise is suitable for you.

We function most powerfully when we are giving love.

Choco Coco Delights

Takes 6 minutes (+ 15 minutes of waiting) | makes 6 pieces

Ingredients

45 grams shredded coconut, 3 tablespoons rice syrup,
6 tablespoons melted extra virgin coconut oil,
15 drops vanilla essence, 1 bag of **YOGI TEA® Choco** (contents)

Preparation

Warm coconut and contents of YOGI TEA® Choco tea bag in a pan on very medium heat for a 3 minutes. Add vanilla, rice syrup and coconut oil. Warm again for 2 minutes turn heat off and place mixture in freezer for 5 minutes. Remove from freezer and shape into rectangular shapes. Put back in freezer for another 10 minutes. Ready to serve.

Ayurvedic Info: V-P-K+

Yoga for Youth and Joy

Sit in easy pose. Make fists of your hands and place them in front of you as if you were grasping a steering wheel. Beginn twisting the body powerfully from side to side. Twist to your maximum. Keep the elbows up and let the neck move with the upper body. Continue for 3 minutes. Then stretch the arms out in front of you. The right hand over the left and the palms are facing down. Twist now from left to right. Move your head and neck in the same direction. Continue coordinating the movement for 3 minutes.

Please ask your doctor if this exercise is suitable for you.

Look within, everything you want is there.

Ginger Orange Vanilla Cookies

Takes 20 minutes (+ soaking time) | makes 5

Ingredients

50 grams rice flour, 20 grams cashews (soaked = 25 grams),
15 grams poppy seeds, pinch baking powder, pinch sea salt,
2 bags of **YOGI TEA® Ginger Orange Vanilla** (contents), 15 drops
of organic vanilla essence, 30 grams rice syrup, 25 grams medjool dates
(without the pit), 8 grams avocado or coconut oil, 15 ml of water

Preparation

*Cover Cashews with water into a bowl and soak for 3–4 hours. Rinse
and strain. Chop. Combine flour, cashews, poppy seeds, baking powder,
sea salt, contents of 2 bags of YOGI TEA® Ginger Orange Vanilla, vanilla
essence, rice syrup, medjool dates, oil and water into a bowl. Use clean
hands to kneed and mix well. Preheat oven to 180 °C. Shape dough into
5 equal balls. Place onto baking sheet covered oven tray. Use palm of hand
to press down and make into disc shaped cookies. Bake for 15 minutes.
Let cool. Serve or store in airtight glass jar.*

Ayurvedic Info: V-P-K+

Dance & Relax

Stand up straight, close your eyes and relax.
Breathe long and deep, feel every tension in your
body and consciously let it go. Sway from side to
side, dance and gently move every part of your
body. If you have soft, rhythmical music, let it
play in the background. Duration: 3–11 minutes.
Please ask your doctor if this exercise is suitable for you.

Happiness is when we realize how blessed we are.

Ginger Orange Vanilla Mango Custard

Takes 10 minutes (+ soaking time) | makes 4 portions

Ingredients

300 grams mango, 80 grams organic dried mango,
200 ml hot water, 4 bags of **YOGI TEA® Ginger Orange Vanilla**,
200 grams coconut milk, 8 teaspoons of arrow root

Preparation

Make tea from hot water (100 °C) and YOGI TEA® tea bags. Steep for 7 – 10 minutes. Remove tea bags. In a bowl, soak dried mango and let soften. When soft: drain and place fresh mango, dried mango, tea, coconut milk in blender (or use hand mixer) and make into cream. Place into pan, let warm for a few minutes to medium low heat until you see vapor rise. Make sure it doesn't boil though. Mix arrow root powder with a little bit of cool water, stir well. Add this mixture to mango cream. Keep stirring while still heating to medium low heat. Stir until you see the cream thicken and firm up. Turn the heat off. Place in bowl, sprinkle with dried coconut grind and mint.

Ayurvedic Info: V-P-K+

Simple Yoga for 'Get Up and Go'

Bundle Roll: Lie on your back, legs together, arms at sides. Flip yourself over from back to stomach and from stomach to back, without bending any part of the body. 3 minutes.

Please ask your doctor if this exercise is suitable for you.

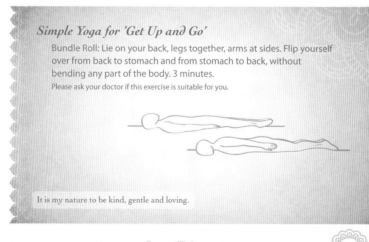

It is my nature to be kind, gentle and loving.

Himalayan Ice-Cream

Takes 5 minutes (not including steeping / freezing time) | makes 4 large portions

Ingredients

400 grams (over)ripe bananas, 100 ml hot water, 4 bags of **YOGI TEA® Himalaya**

Preparation

Let tea steep in hot water (100°C) for 20 minutes or so. Remove the bags and let it cool. Remove the skin of the banana and cut in small pieces. Place tea and banana in Tupperware in freezer for at least 5 hours. Take out just before use. Let defrost for a minute, chop in pieces using a knife. Use a hand mixer to make this mix into a frozen cream. Serve immediately.

Ayurvedic Info: V-P-Ko

Simple Yoga for Balancing and Strenghtening the Body

Be on hands and knees. Raise left leg and right arm (keep straight). Hold 3 minutes. Inhale and raise opposite arm and leg. Hold 2.5 minutes.

Please ask your doctor if this exercise is suitable for you.

With every step you take be aware of all the things you do.

Rooibos Maple Sticky Cake

Takes 35 minutes | makes 4 portions

Ingredients

50 grams brown rice flour, 25 grams shredded coconut,
6 grams baking powder, 2 pinches of sea salt,
120 grams ripe banana, 3 bags of **YOGI TEA® Rooibos** (contents),
4 tablespoons maple syrup, 2 tablespoons palm sugar,
2 ½ tablespoons liquid coconut oil

Preparation

Combine all ingredients in a bowl. Use fork to mash banana well and mix in with other ingredients. Place into cake tin. Preheat oven to 180 °C. Bake cake for 30 minutes. Let cool.

Ayurvedic Info: V-P-K+

Simple Yoga to take away stress

Sit on your heels and rest the upper body on the thighs, forehead on the ground. Pat your lower back rhythmically with your hands in a slow relaxing rhythm. 2–3 minutes.

Please ask your doctor if this exercise is suitable for you.

To be beautiful means to be yourself.

Muesli Energy Bars

Takes 10 minutes (+ 30 minutes freezer time) | makes 4

Ingredients

30 grams oat flakes, 30 grams pumpkin seeds,
30 grams hemp seeds, 20 grams cacao butter, 4 tablespoons rice syrup, 1½ – 2 bags of **YOGI TEA® Women's
Energy** (contents), 10 drops vanilla essence (optional)

Preparation

*Let the cacao butter melt in a pan over medium heat. Add rice syrup,
essence, contents of 1½ to 2 bags of YOGI TEA® Women's Energy tea. Stir
well. Add oat flakes and hemp seeds. Stir well. Place in the freezer for 10 to
15 minutes. Take out and with hands shape into 2 rectangular bars. Place
into freezer for another 10 – 15 minutes. Wrap in baking paper. Store or serve.*
Tip: *Store these bars in an airtight glass jar and they keep for a few weeks.*

Ayurvedic Info: V-P-K+

Grasshopper Pose

Lay flat on the ground on a pad or rug, belly to the floor. Bring your
hands into fists. Slide the fists between your body and the floor, just
above the pelvic bones. Keeping the legs together, raise them as high
as possible. The chin and torso stay in contact with the
floor. Hold the position for 1–3 minutes, breathing
slowly and deeply. Relax. (Locust Pose is believed
to aid digestion by circulating energy through
the stomach and intestines and is thought to tone
abdominal muscles.)

Please ask your doctor if this
exercise is suitable for you.

Affirm your faith and not your doubt.

Enjoy!

With great joy YOGI TEA® presents healthy and ayurvedic recipes for your inspiration. The base for the wonderful recipes in this book has the same composition as our teas. Age-old healing traditions in the oriental environment of spices have made them an important element in countless dishes and beverages in a unique way.

You will find them in YOGI TEA® and in this recipe book.

We wish you an inspiring and delightful time as well as a glorious new taste experience with our spicy teas and dishes.

Please send your feedback on your experience with this cookbook, photos as well as your own recipes, to share on our website and on our facebook page.

www.yogitea.eu